Josiah's Sanctification

Lessons Learned from a Lost Book

Thomas Murosky, Ph.D.

Kings of All Creation Series Vol 1

Our Walk In Christ Publishing
State College, PA

© 2019 by Thomas Murosky, Ph.D.

Published by Our Walk in Christ Publishing
State College, PA
www.owicpub.com

All rights reserved. No part of this publication may be reproduced, distributed, or transmitted in any form or by any means, including photocopying, recording, or other electronic or mechanical methods, without the prior written permission of the publisher, except in the case of brief quotations embodied in critical reviews and certain other noncommercial uses permitted by copyright law.

Josiah's Sanctification: Lessons Learned from a Lost Book

First Printing 2019
ISBN: 978-1-7325696-4-5 (sc)
ISBN: 978-1-7325696-5-2 (e)

Scripture quotations taken from the New American Standard Bible® (NASB), Copyright © 1960, 1962, 1963, 1968, 1971, 1972, 1973, 1975, 1977, 1995 by The Lockman Foundation. Used by permission. www.lockman.org

The Internet addresses in this book are accurate at the time of publication. They are provided as a resource, but due to the nature of the Internet, those addresses may change.

Commitment to Open Source: Our Walk in Christ Publishing uses FOSS software where available. This book was produced with LibreOffice, GNU Image Manipulator Program, Sigil, and the following open fonts: Charis SIL, PlainBlack, and DejaVu Sans. Chapter dividers obtained from https://openclipart.org. Audiobook edition produced with Audacity and Kid3.

LCCN: 2019939407

Dedication

The following study of Josiah, his kingdom, and the applications drawn from his life is dedicated to Dr. Jim Nolten, the pastor of the first church I joined after becoming a Christian. It was his sermon on this subject which so radically transformed my views on sanctification and practical Christian living.

Acknowledgments

I wish to acknowledge my followers and readers in the online communities for the encouragement to continue writing and teaching across the spectrum of the Christian faith. Thanks for watching and reading. Please stay in touch!

I also wish to acknowledge my financial backers who provide the support allowing me to spend more time researching, learning, and writing on these topics.

Thanks also to the beta readers for the initial thoughts on the manuscript before publication, and to Kate for doing the initial round of editing.

Finally thanks to you, my readers, who make putting my thoughts on paper and digital ink worth the while! I pray that my experiences while growing in my faith over will help you grow as you walk in Christ.

Table of Contents

Introduction	7
Learning Objectives	11
Josiah: A Conflicted Kingdom	23
The Incubation Period	35
The Written Word	49
Changing Hearts	59
Planning to Grow	75
Create Your Personal Plan	89
The Gospel	93
Scripture Index	96

Introduction

My first experience inside in a church building was somehow connected to a day care of some sort when I was scantly a toddler. It was a one-off thing, a playgroup or something. I remember the big stained glass windows and the old toys, but nothing more. My family were not believers. My father was raised Catholic and my mother was from a Protestant breed of some form or another. My father's priest asked why he would want to marry a Protestant wh@#$ when the subject of marriage arose. You can imagine my parents never thought much of God, and their thoughts became my thoughts.

I never lived with my father but my mom ran off with a boyfriend when I was yet a baby and they married out of threat of separation, but such a relationship did not last so we traveled back across the country to my mother's home state and lived with relatives until she could get a job and a place of our own. That was just before Easter in the 1980's, so we attended a service like the rest of the small town as was expected in most small town communities in America at that time.

At the service we stood singing common Easter songs and hearing a boring guy say things I did not understand but I asked my mom who God is. The reply was short and simple: I do not know and don't ask again! Such was my upbringing in this world.

I tell this story so you understand I was not a person raised in a church hearing those songs that 'everyone knows' or confessing Jesus from an early age out of peer pressure or to please a parent or Sunday school teacher. I am thankful for my upbringing however odd that may be because it allowed me to go into my Christian walk in total ignorance. Such ignorance is a great blessing if you have the humility to understand it, and if there is anything I understood at the end of my undergraduate years and the start of my graduate studies, it is how woefully ignorant all of us are in life!

This seriously helped my Christian walk because I was not converted by a church member, or a friend, or a family member, or some alter call. I wrestled with God and lost the match. Jesus rode into my evil, black, vulgar heart, kicked out the demons and set up camp. I belonged to Him. No church was my influence, no friend pressured me. In fact, most of the people who spent long hours praying for my salvation had no knowledge I was saved until several months or even years later. Those prayers for my salvation by my oldest friends were not uttered in vain.

But this conversion meant I had no direction in my life but a Bible. The sword in the hands of an academic scholar meant I filtered everything through the pages of Scripture above all, and was not beholden to the teachings of Churchianity. But it also meant I had no idea what I was doing in the faith. I sat down to read the Bible that was collecting dust on my bookshelf since my high school biology teacher had given it to me five years prior. I dusted it off and cracked open that cover to find a rich land of powerful literature.

About nine months later I read enough to learn church is very important, so I started attending services and learning from the sermons, Sunday school classes, and also by reading great books about the Bible.

After about two years of growth my pastor preached a great sermon on King Josiah and the message changed something within me. It taught about sanctification, growth in the Lord, and letting go of worldly things to follow God instead.

That day I deleted files from my computer, destroyed old movies, tossed out music, and even went through sentimental items disposing of a lot of things that while not evil, were certainly locking me into my wretched past, preventing me from moving forward into the future.

I pray this short study on King Josiah will give you such boldness and confidence to let go of the sin in your past and move forward to a better life with Christ as defined by the pages of Holy Scripture.

1
Learning Objectives

As we approach Scripture in our personal studies and devotions, we should always be in prayer asking God to bless our efforts by showing us our sin, faults, and our means of improvement. Consider the prayer of King David in *Psalm 139*:

> *Search me, O God, and know my heart;*
> *Try me and know my anxious thoughts;*
> *And see if there be any hurtful way in me,*
> *And lead me in the everlasting way.*
> *(Psalm 139:23-24)*

How To Grow In Faith

Our task as a Christian is to grow in Christ. Paul declares in *1 Thessalonians 4:3* that the will of God is our sanctification. The doctrine of sanctification is difficult for many people because it is the step of our faith we directly participate in. While we do not like to talk much about predestination, it is true God the Father ordains our salvation, and even our justification is not dependent on ourselves...and that is good because we are prone to wander as sheep. If left to our own devices we would wander off into strange pastures leading to personal condemnation.

But as saved people, how we live our life *is* up to us. I am not preaching a 'Carnal Christian' life nor Easy Believism, and I affirm some people get so caught up in emotional Gospel presentations they pray a prayer outwardly but are not truly saved. Real Christians, those who genuinely come to faith, will hunger and thirst after the Word as a deer pants for water brooks (*Psalm 42:1-2*). The true Christian longs to dive into the Word, to let it permeate their heart, and to be transformed by the God of the universe. **In short, our first learning objective is to Start Following Jesus Christ.**

Learning Objectives

Christians understand the need to follow Jesus, but even that topic has been convoluted over the years. Many different teachings have arisen about who Jesus is, what He did or said, and what true worship means. Some churches fully embrace the world while others decry anything from the world as evil. Christendom has become as confusing to a new believer as rocket science is to the masses! Others hear popular but damning messages about being sincere in your faith above all, and that all roads lead to heaven (*John 14:6*). Be assured, God has not left us to navigate these minefields alone (*2 Timothy 3:16*). The objective standard for what pleases God is the Bible, so **our second learning objective is to discover the Word of God.**

Some denominations want to say God has audibly spoken to them. While I will not put God in a box to say He cannot choose to do that, it is not the general practice for how He works in this New Testament age. We are not supposed to run around seeking special messages, and many who make such messages a priority in their life often fall to ruin as they do not vet the source and so hear instead from demons (*2 Corinthians 11:4*). But God speaks very clearly through the pages of Scripture making it the best place to hear His message to us. It is through the pages of Scripture we hear from God, and so **our third object is to hear from God through the Bible.**

Our final objective deals with how we live our life. There is a rumor out there that a person can say a little prayer and be eternally saved no matter what else happens. Such a formula gives false hope to people who want to see their loved ones in heaven even though they do not live out their life in obedience to God (*John 14:15*). While our salvation is a free gift that is not in any way dependent on our works, the works we do as Christians are a mark we are actually saved. In this, it is up to us to spend time devoting ourselves to Christ and transforming our life in a way which is pleasing to Him. **Our final learning objective in this book is to bring your life into obedience to the Scriptures.**

Learning Objectives

Preparation

As we prepare to dive into this study on the life of Josiah, we need to be prepared. We will need our textbook: the Bible. Also, keep a notebook or two handy. Some paper for notes and some for prayers. Have your writing instruments ready and find a quiet place to study free of distractions.

Bible

It is important to find a good Bible you can read and understand. In the world of Christianity there are some debates always arising about which translations are the best and which are not. I understand this debate but also stay a bit aloof from it because of the fruitless arguments, and some people declare that all modern translations are bad. I do not agree.

First we will find the King James Version only crowd. These people want to decry every modern translation is perverted and written to teach doctrines of demons. That is simply not true. The King James Version is a decent translation, but I do not recommend it for most people because the language

Josiah's Sanctification

and stylings is out of date with our present dialog. You see, languages evolve as they are being used, and the text the KJV Bible heralds from was written in England in 1611. Words have come and gone, sentence structure and spellings have changed, and the feel of the book is old, so in 1769 an edited version arose which corrected a few errors in the original 1611 version and this is what we now know as the King James or Authorized Version. Despite what is said from people in this crowd, there is nothing specifically holier about the KJV Bible. There was no angel who handed down the translation, rather it was the product of studied men of God living in that era.

But the people on the opposite spectrum often declare the Bible to be full of *old ideas*, and these ideas merit editing. Some modern translations do actually attempt to change the meaning of some texts, leave out some doctrines, or ignore some interpretations. These translations give credit to the KJV only crowd, but that is not the case with all modern translations.

Some modern translations are better because archaeological findings have discovered older and more accurate manuscripts which were not available to the translators in 1611 when that edition was translated. Further, more classical Greek texts have increased our understanding of the texts written in the original Greek language so new translations not only have presented the text in our modern language, but also with a better understanding of some passages.

That being said, we have too many translations and I am under the impression we need to stop making new English Bibles and focus on reading and studying the ones we have. So my final takeaway here is if you have a Bible you like, keep it and study it. If you are in the market to buy a Bible, I recommend one of the following:

NASB: New American Standard Bible

ESV: English Standard Version

HCSB: Holman Christian Standard Bible

NKJV: New King James Version

While there may be other Bibles that are fine, I would stick to these as they have good reputations, are translated by biblically sound organizations, and have widespread acceptance among some of the best Bible teachers of our day.

Paper

It is important to actually talk about paper and notebooks since our modern world has taught us to do everything on computers.

My first career out of graduate school was a college professor, and this was right when digital technology was being introduced as the revolutionary new way to grade student homework. The promise they gave us was to assign all the work we wanted but we did not need to take the time to grade papers, so everything was perfect! But it was not. We quickly found out students may have been submitting more work than before, but their understanding generally decreased! The reason is simple: it is the process that teaches us, not the answer. The homework solutions graded answers, but could not discern whether a student followed the process that could help them learn. This reinforced bad habits of getting final answers fast, which reflected poorly on their understanding.

We find similar results when taking notes on a computer. You can have all the notes in clean text, searchable fields, color-coded to perfection, but a problem arises in such a notation system: it only gives us recognition, not understanding. In a psychology text on knowledge and learning, Howard University professor Max Meenes wrote about study habits[1]. Knowledge, he says, can be confused with recognition. In his research he says the first phase of learning is recognition. Do you recognize the answer when you see it, or can you discern the right answer from similar wrong answers? This is the lowest level of knowledge. Next, he says there is memorization, which is to be able to recite lists or phrases. This often does not lead to understanding anything, which is sad because this is the type of teaching we often give our children in their Sunday school classes and related Christian activities. The final means of knowledge is understanding, which allows us to put together new information with what we already know. We can recall that information and put it into practice. When we understand what we are learning, we can actively apply it to our life.

When you know what Professor Meenes is saying, you understand why digital note taking does not solve any problems: it is all about recognition, never about understanding.

Further in his research he talks about how to make understanding occur and it is of no surprise that it is through the process of writing. Ask any English teacher: essays always tell you a lot more about whether a student knows the subject than true/false, multiple choice, or fill in the blank. It is because you need to understand to do the essay. Meenes finds in his research that students gain understanding by writing on paper, mostly through muscle memory.

Not only do you want to take down notes when you are studying, but you also want to take down prayers. Prayer is a means of grace by which we learn who God is, and when we write down our prayers and the ways God answers them, we can better understand how He is working in our life.

Learning Objectives

A Quiet Place

It is important to find a time and a place for our personal studies. Some people love the morning hours. Many parents have said the early hours before kids arise is the best time for their devotions. Other's prefer evenings. The time is not as important as the schedule. For me, it has shifted over the years. As an early graduate student, I found the evenings best. I came home from work, grabbed the Bible and books and set out for a coffee shop to spend an hour or two reading, writing, and praying. Those were some of the best days for my Christian growth. After a few years, time was more demanding and I found myself at the lab in the mornings and evenings, so I shifted my Bible time to my lunch hour. In those days I would take an hour of time, go off somewhere quiet with my study materials and focus on God during my lunch break. As a professor, my time necessarily shifted to the morning hours. I would get up every morning about an hour before I needed to leave for the university and get my reading in so I did not need to 'find a time' to get the study in between office hours, labs, and grading papers.

Chapter Summary

This chapter we discussed the learning objectives for this book. They are **Start Following Jesus Christ**, **Rediscover the Bible**, **Learn to Hear from God**, and **Transform Your Life**.

To get ready to study this book, have a Bible you can read and understand, a notebook, and a quiet comfortable place to learn. Start with prayer and ask God to teach you in each section.

2
Josiah: A Conflicted Kingdom

*I will completely remove all things from the face of the
earth, I will remove man and beast;
I will remove the birds of the sky
And the fish of the sea,
And the ruins along with the wicked;
And I will cut off man from the face of the earth.
So I will stretch out My hand against Judah
And against all the inhabitants of Jerusalem.
And I will cut off the remnant of Baal from this place,
And the names of the idolatrous
priests along with the priests.
And those who bow down on the
housetops to the host of heaven,
And those who bow down and swear
to the LORD and yet swear by Milcom,
And those who have turned back
from following the LORD,
And those who have not sought the*

Josiah's Sanctification

LORD or inquired of Him.
(Zephaniah 1:2-6)

Josiah inherited a wretched mess from his pagan father. Not unlike my own childhood with parents who knew nothing of God, Josiah likely grew up doing whatever was right in his own eyes (*Judges 21:25*). In the final accounting of his days, however, we know Josiah *did right in the sight of the Lord, and walked in the ways of his father David (2 Chronicles 34:2)*. Despite his upbringing and examples, Josiah overcame the pagan upbringing to become a king praised by God. Was this merely the influence of the priest, Hilkiah? Probably not for reasons we will examine at the end of this chapter. But to understand Josiah and what we can learn from his life, we need to go back a few generations.

Josiah was one of the last kings of the southern kingdom. Under Saul, David, and Solomon, Israel was a united kingdom of twelve tribes, but idolatry and other sins divided the kingdom causing the Israelites to split into two nations. The northern kingdom took the name Israel and did not have any righteous or

Josiah: A Conflicted Kingdom

repentant kings. They were judged by God quickly, conquered and carried off into exile by the Assyrians in 722 BC.

The southern kingdom took the name Judah and had a few righteous and repentant kings in their history, although many of the kings still did evil in the site of the Lord. Josiah's great grandfather was Hezekiah, the righteous king who kept Jerusalem from Assyrian captivity by his prayers to God. The prophet Isaiah was an adviser to his kingdom and proclaimed the message of delivery to the King when Sennacherib invaded Judah (*Isaiah 36-37*).

Hezekiah reformed Judah by removing the high places of worship, destroying the idols including the bronze serpent Moses made in the wilderness (*Numbers 21:6-9*; the people of Judah named it Nahushtan and worshiped it), and cutting down the Asherah also used in pagan worship. Hezekiah held firmly to the Lord through the trials against Assyria and for that trust in God over the Assyrian control we, are told there were no other kings like him before or since (*2 Kings 18:5*).

Josiah's Sanctification

As Hezekiah passed away, his son Manasseh became king in his place and he was such a wicked king it was like he was making up for the years of lost idol worship. Manasseh rebuilt the high places and established a cult of Baal worship such as was only seen in the north. Further, Manasseh defiled the temple by bringing idols into it. The prophets warned Manasseh but he did not listen, they warned the people, but neither did they listen. The judgment was set:

> *But they did not listen, and Manasseh seduced them to do evil more than the nations whom the LORD destroyed before the sons of Israel (2 Kings 21:9).*

Manasseh repented in captivity at the very end of his life, but it was not enough to placate the impending judgment. Manasseh died and his son Amon became king in his place. Amon was equally wicked continuing the worship established by his father, but he was assassinated after two years and his son, Josiah, became the king in his place.

Josiah: A Conflicted Kingdom

So Josiah inherits a kingdom worshiping in every way God had forbidden. He was the grandson of two generations of the most wicked kings Judah had ever known. The message of destruction from Zephaniah was written during Josiah's kingdom, a warning of the impending doom over the nation.

Josiah Follows God

Now that we have our context for the kingdom during Josiah's reign, we can learn how a child born of wickedness came the closest to reforming the kingdom according to Moses's law. Start by reading *2 Chronicles 34:1-3*:

> *Josiah was eight years old when he became king, and he reigned thirty-one years in Jerusalem. He did right in the sight of the LORD, and walked in the ways of his father David and did not turn aside to the right or to the left. For in the eighth year of his reign while he was still a youth, he began to seek the God of his father David; and in the twelfth year he began to purge Judah and Jerusalem of the high places, the Asherim, the carved images and the molten images.*

Josiah's Sanctification

The Boy King

It was not completely unusual for a child to be a king but I want to focus on something else here. Notice that he was eight when he became king, but in the eighth year of his reign he began seeking God. This means he was sixteen before he started following God, so we are left to assume the pagan worship established in his grandfather's reign was still being conducted, maybe even by Josiah himself.

We do not know much about his reign or the policies during this period, but we know the kingdom was ignoring the prophets sent to warn them about following God and that the other prophets were lying about what God said (*Zephaniah 3:4*). We also know people still relied on priests to offer sacrifices and those were being done on the high places throughout the land. Even though Josiah was being informed by priests, it is likely they were as blind as the king himself (*Zephaniah 3:4*).

Then Josiah, at the age of sixteen, starts seeking God. We do not have any indication about what caused him to draw near to God, but it may have to do with the prophet Zephaniah.

Zephaniah is a relative of Josiah, also tracing his lineage back to Hezekiah (*Zephaniah 1:1*). He was also a prophet in Jerusalem and seemed to preach before Josiah's reforms. It was likely he had an audience in the king due to being in the royal bloodline and his preaching to the young Josiah caused him to see the dangers of following in his forefather's footsteps. Such warnings are the possible cause of Josiah's repentance.

To Grow In Christ

Repentance happens when God transforms our heart in response to the Gospel. Our task as Christians is to preach the Gospel to everyone. We are not called to convert people, but merely to preach. *1 Corinthians* elucidates this principle:

> *I planted, Apollos watered, but God was causing the growth. So then neither the one who plants nor the one who waters is anything, but God who causes the growth (1 Corinthians 3:6-7).*

The people in Corinth were producing small sects among each other saying to be of the sect of Paul and of the sect of Apollos, but Paul corrects their theology that it is God who causes growth. We are to preach the Gospel; that is our role:

> How then will they call on Him in whom they have not believed? How will they believe in Him whom they have not heard? And how will they hear without a preacher? How will they preach unless they are sent? Just as it is written, "HOW BEAUTIFUL ARE THE FEET OF THOSE WHO BRING GOOD NEWS OF GOOD THINGS! (Romans 10:14-15)"

The preaching of the Gospel is called the **General Call** in theology and that call is the groundwork God uses to call someone to Himself. Once we come to Him, He transforms our heart and makes us fertile to learn from His word.

Taken together, it was the preaching of Zephaniah which laid the groundwork in Josiah's heart to make him seek God, but he had a problem in that no one had seen the Book of the Law in at least a few generations. This is why I believe Hilkiah and the other priests were sincere about following God but they were not able to advise the king in matters of the Law.

Present Application

I observe two applications we can draw from this short section of Scripture. First, Josiah was likely the product of his generation and likewise we are the product of ours. I opened with some personal testimony as it was important to understand the way I grew up seemed very normal to me, and the way you grew up seems very normal to you. Psychologists speak of a *Family of Origin* meaning however we grow up, we think that to be normal. In some dysfunctional families, the kids are raised into warped thinking. To help people recognize what is believed to be healthy, one husband-wife counselor team wrote a book about how to teach people what normal is[2], well, at least what normal is to them!

Like Josiah, we may think our life growing up is honoring to God, but it may not be. Pray for God to reveal to you, from the Word, whether or not your experiences are in alignment with the Word. Spend some time praying over key passages of Scripture to see if your walk with God is honoring to Him.

Josiah's Sanctification

Second, we believe Josiah likely heard the impending judgment on his kingdom from Zephaniah. This could be a foreshadowing of the Gospel. We are tasked with The Great Commission to preach to the whole world making disciples. It is clear from *1 Corinthians* we are not to make sects of the Christian faith, but to sow and water while letting God decide who grows and where.

Also remember like from my story, there were several people in my life preaching the Gospel to me and praying for my salvation. I came to Jesus at His timing, in His place, and without the further direct intervention of those wonderful friends! Here are a couple of applications about my conversion: first, keep praying and preaching, but second, do not be alarmed if your friends do not bow their knees to Jesus right when you want them to.

Chapter Summary

Josiah inherited a mess from his fathers, and for a period of time it remained in the same fallen state. In response to preaching from Zephaniah he turned to God in the only way he knew how.

As believers today, we are tasked with preaching. Like Zephaniah, preach wherever you will be heard. Do not be concerned about bringing people to Jesus; accept some people will never come to Christ but others will come when He has deemed ready. Keep praying at all times, and remember the effective prayer of a righteous man accomplishes much (*James 5:16*).

3
The Incubation Period

Then it will come about on the
day of the LORD'S sacrifice
That I will punish the princes, the king's sons
And all who clothe themselves with foreign garments.
And I will punish on that day
all who leap on the temple threshold,
Who fill the house of their lord
with violence and deceit.
On that day there will be the sound
of a cry from the Fish Gate,
A wail from the Second Quarter,
And a loud crash from the hills.
Wail, O inhabitants of the Mortar,
For all the people of Canaan will be silenced;
All who weigh out silver will be cut off.
It will come about at that time
That I will search Jerusalem with lamps,
And I will punish the men who are stagnant in spirit,
Who say in their hearts,

Josiah's Sanctification

'The LORD will not do good or evil!'
(Zephaniah 1:8-12)

Josiah's path to God is not a lot different from most of us. He heard a message, repented and started following God, and then had to learn what that really meant.

In our day, it can be difficult to understand what the Gospel actually means because recent years have seen many well meaning preachers try to create a formula to get people to become a Christian. One theology professor even wrote an article in the *Christian Post* recently which talks about removing difficult parts from the Gospel message[3]. While I agreed with many of his assertions, a few of them were clearly problematic to the Christian faith. Most notably, he does not want us to tell people the Bible is the inerrant Word of God!

His method is understandable, but faulty. He wants to make sure people are not scared away from the Gospel by something that is hard to hear, but this approach is the complete opposite of what Jesus told us to preach:

The Incubation Period

Now large crowds were going along with Him; and He turned and said to them, "If anyone comes to Me, and does not hate his own father and mother and wife and children and brothers and sisters, yes, and even his own life, he cannot be My disciple. Whoever does not carry his own cross and come after Me cannot be My disciple. For which one of you, when he wants to build a tower, does not first sit down and calculate the cost to see if he has enough to complete it? Otherwise, when he has laid a foundation and is not able to finish, all who observe it begin to ridicule him, saying, 'This man began to build and was not able to finish.' Or what king, when he sets out to meet another king in battle, will not first sit down and consider whether he is strong enough with ten thousand men to encounter the one coming against him with twenty thousand? Or else, while the other is still far away, he sends a delegation and asks for terms of peace. So then, none of you can be My disciple who does not give up all his own possessions (Luke 14:25-33).

This is difficult to hear, but hear it we must. To become a Christian is a hard task; we must count the cost and pay it. Josiah had started counting. He counted not only the cost of salvation but the cost of failing to be saved! His nation was under the thumb of

Josiah's Sanctification

God and he had to act. Let's once again notice another part of his story:

> *For in the eighth year of his reign while he was still a youth, he began to seek the God of his father David; and in the twelfth year he began to purge Judah and Jerusalem of the high places, the Asherim, the carved images and the molten images (2 Chronicles 34:3).*

We first looked at this verse in the last chapter, but I wanted to look at another part of it here. Notice this sixteen year old king begins seeking the Lord, but it is not until he is twenty when he actually starts purifying the kingdom. We will talk about the purification part later, but what was happening during this period?

I have a few theories, but they are only that. First, I liken this to the time period between when I first became a Christian and the period of time when I started my ministry for God. There was a lag of about four years when I was dealing with the fallout of my dysfunctional upbringing and learning what it was to be a Christian. I spent time learning who I was by reading the Bible. My time in Scripture showed me

The Incubation Period

how my life was wretchedly evil and how I needed to rethink even the most foundational presuppositions of my life. I took the time to learn what made me grow into the sinner I was from a practical standpoint.

The reason I only propose this as a theory for Josiah's life is he did not have the complete canon of the Bible but we do. He did have some priests and prophets who knew God, but that was confounded by others who practiced evil in God's sight. There was no objective standard except the preaching of some prophets, but again, other prophets were delivering conflicting messages.

Another theory is he was indeed learning about God from a prophet who knew Him, perhaps even Zephaniah himself. We just do not know because we have little information about either the prophet or the king during this growth period. Whatever was happening, however, it is clear Josiah was changed and earnestly sought to follow God.

Josiah's Sanctification

Time To Grow

Regardless of what was going on in Josiah's heart and how, it is important to note the lag in time between when he started following God and when he really started to please God in his actions. I call this period of time the **Incubation Period**.

Most Christians I know have had a period of time when they first became Christians and when their life really looks like they are saved. As I said in the first chapter, I completely and vehemently deny the concept of a 'Carnal Christian' which some circles have called a person who does not live like a Christian but is really saved based on a prayer they said in their past. But I do affirm a new believer will not instantly become mature.

Liken this, if you will, to a child growing up. When a baby is born, he is unable to feed himself, use facilities, or walk. A baby will also cram anything you give it into its mouth. We do not expect a baby to pop out and become a mature adult. It takes a long time of faithful nurturing.

The Incubation Period

Likewise, it takes a long time of growth for a baby Christian to become a mature believer. In this growth stage, like a child, the Christian needs to be fed, nurtured, and guided. Like we teach our kids what to eat and what not to eat, we mentor Christians in the faith of sound doctrine and theology. We teach them to feed themselves and grow, to think, and make good decisions. That is the model for Christian growth.

So what is the difference between one of these immature Christians and a 'Carnal Christian'? It is a matter of nurture. A person who has no interest in the things of God, no desire to grow, no desire to pray or read the Word, no desire for growth and fellowship is simply not a Christian! The fact you may have said a prayer does not make you saved. Yes, I know the verse that says:

If you confess with your mouth Jesus as Lord and believe in your heart that God raised him from the dead, you will be saved (Romans 10:9).

The problem is our one-verse church culture teaching streamlined evangelism will not allow for someone to read that verse in context to complete the sentence:

For with the heart a person believes, resulting in righteousness, and with the mouth he confesses, resulting in salvation (Romans 10:10).

The mouth and confession is salvation, but if salvation has come to your heart, the result will be righteousness. A person who does not grow is simply not saved. But a person who hungers after the Word will grow in faith!

How To Follow God

A challenge we have at this point is put to a simple question: What does it mean to follow God? We have the benefit of the Bible while Josiah did not. He was responding to the message in Zephaniah's prophesy:

*So I will stretch out My hand against Judah
And against all the inhabitants of Jerusalem.
And I will cut off the remnant of Baal from this place,
And the names of the idolatrous
priests along with the priests.
And those who bow down on the
housetops to the host of heaven,
And those who bow down and swear to the LORD and
yet swear by Milcom, And those who have turned back*

> *from following the LORD,*
> *And those who have not sought*
> *the LORD or inquired of Him.*
> *(Zephaniah 1:4-6)*

We see here the Baal worship, idolatry, worship outside the temple, swearing by other Gods. If this was the message he responded to, the logical thing to do is remove these activities from the kingdom! But within a few more years, more clarity came from the prophet Jeremiah. He received his commission to preach to Judah starting in the thirteenth year of Josiah's reign. Now we have two prophets informing the king about what needs to be done!

We read what the king did in the next section of *2 Chronicles 34:4-7*:

> *They tore down the altars of the Baals in his presence, and the incense altars that were high above them he chopped down; also the Asherim, the carved images and the molten images he broke in pieces and ground to powder and scattered it on the graves of those who had sacrificed to them. Then he burned the bones of the priests on their altars and purged Judah and Jerusalem. In the cities of Manasseh, Ephraim, Simeon, even as far as Naphtali, in their surrounding ruins, he also tore down the altars and beat the Asherim and the*

Josiah's Sanctification

carved images into powder, and chopped down all the incense altars throughout the land of Israel.

The king is busy. In response to the prophecy he started exactly where he was without needing more instruction. He removed the Baal worship, the Asherim, the false priests, and he did so all throughout his kingdom.

Remove Your Sins

The king knew what he had to do without being commanded and often in our life, so do we. God has written His law on our heart (*Hebrews 10:16*). Even before being saved we have a general idea about what is right and what is wrong in the eyes of God. Our conscience is our guide in these matters, though sin can dull it over years of disobedience. However, once we are saved, our conscience is given a megaphone and we regain back most of what we have dulled. Our task then is to do the next logical steps and remove the stumbling blocks to our growth.

If you find yourself a new Christian and addicted to some substance, quit! Get help as needed, be it counseling, fellowship, or some other intervention. If your life is full of false objects of worship like elements used in Wicca or other occultism, get rid of those objects (*Acts 19:18-19*).

Sometimes as believers, we need to cast off some friends, though I always advise to do this cautiously. We are not commanded to have no friendships with unbelievers, but if such friends do interfere with our growth in the Lord, it may be best to place those on the back burner for a while.

In my case as I said in the introduction, I needed to delete some computer files, get rid of some movies and music, and also rid my book collection of some things teaching wrong theologies.

The House Of Worship

Josiah recognized the importance of the temple and sought to clean it. His grandfather, Manasseh brought Baal worship and other idolatrous materials into the temple, but he would be the one to clear it out. In the eighteenth year of his reign when he was 26 years old he issued a command to clean the temple. He appointed three men to oversee the cleaning and rebuilding that the holy sanctuary would once again be honoring to God.

We have to imagine the state of the temple was not anywhere near the glory of the structure when Solomon had completed it. Several decades earlier, Hezekiah stripped the gold from the temple to pay a ransom to Assyria (*2 Kings 18:16*) and no king until Josiah repaired the temple.

In his reign, however, money was collected specifically to clean and repair the temple. At this point, they did not have any frame of reference for what should go into proper worship, yet they worked diligently to seek to honor God. We will see in the next chapter, such sincere worship is not equated with acceptable worship before God.

Start To Follow God Where You Are

The chief lesson we have learned from Josiah in this chapter is to **follow God where you are**. God will fill in the gaps when we seek to honor Him. Josiah up to this point turns to God in response to a message of destruction. He goes through his incubation period and comes out the other side on fire to purify Judah. We need to learn these lessons.

If you have come to this point and have not believed in Jesus, I will call on you to do that now. Do you recognize your sin and see your inability to do anything about it? Then you need Jesus, born of a virgin, and going to the cross willingly for your sins. Believe He was raised from the dead for your sins and place your trust in Him. Once you do that, seek to honor Him in your life by following the Bible.

Your next steps are to begin removing known sin from your life and pray for God to search you throughout and show you any wrong ways in your heart. Once you do that, you are ready to tackle more sin in your life.

Chapter Summary

This chapter carries the first message: **start following God where you are**. We will see in the next chapter Josiah does not yet have the clear directives from God, but he is still honoring God by cleaning the temple, which is the object of destruction as recorded

Josiah's Sanctification

by Zephaniah and Jeremiah. He followed a warning from these prophets and chose to do the opposite and God called him a good king.

4
The Written Word

Therefore wait for Me,
For the day when I rise up as a witness.
Indeed, My decision is to gather nations,
To assemble kingdoms,
To pour out on them My indignation,
All My burning anger;
For all the earth will be devoured
By the fire of My zeal.
For then I will give to the peoples purified lips,
That all of them may call on the name of the LORD,
To serve Him shoulder to shoulder.
(Zephaniah 3:8-9)

It was a warm June evening in the desert where I lived during my last teaching post. At the end of the school year our science department always had a final party as we parted ways. Our institutional contracts were nine months on with the entire summer

Josiah's Sanctification

as a fully paid vacation and it was the last time most of us would have seen one another until the mandatory meetings in mid-August to kick off the new academic year. Our most senior professor always opened up his home for the party. His mother was the 'grandmother' figure of the first church I joined in that town and this man walked 'all paths of truth' with his radical Christian upbringing and his Buddhist wife.

The rest of the guests had left for home and it was just me, our host, and a man from Sri Lanka. Our host was highly impacted by my direct faith during the interview a few years prior when my hiring committee consisted of an atheist, a Catholic who walked away from the faith, a practicing witch, and our vice president (who may have been a vampire...he had an allergic reaction to the sun!). The atheist, who cared not for procedure as he was called in out of retirement to take over until someone was hired, saw all the Christian activity on my CV and asked the illegal question: *Would you proselytize our students?*

The Vice President, horrified, retorted, "You can't ask that!" but I calmed the room and offered an answer which was graciously stolen from Chip Ingram:

> As a Christian I need to obey authority, which is you. The laws would not allow me to use my classroom for evangelism and being a secular institution, I am bound by my God to obey that. But let me assure you, if a student came to my office with a personal problem and asked my opinion, I would certainly offer Jesus Christ as a possible solution.

Our party host was floored by that answer and he told me of that not long after, but during this June evening with a Sri Lankan man, the conversation turned to faith. I asserted the stance that there is only one path to God, and the man from across the globe had some great questions. But the host held different beliefs even suggesting the often heard statement, "It does not matter what one believes as long as he is sincere!" So is that statement true? Are the beliefs we hold all equally valid, and it is just our sincerity that grants us entrance into heaven? I do not think so, and we will let another lesson from Josiah explain.

Josiah's Sanctification

The Inadequate Cleanup

Up to this point in time we have seen Josiah start following God. He spent the first eight years of his reign probably adhering to the pagan practices his father handed down, but then the Lord called. After a few years on this path, he saw the need to clean up the kingdom and the temple as we have seen.

We know Josiah had great sincerity in his faith. He took God seriously in response to the messages of destruction from both Zephaniah and Jeremiah. He knew that to continue the path his fathers taught him was destruction, and he did the best that came to his mind: cleanse the land of the things the prophets warned them about!

Josiah was very sincere, but that was not enough. He had commissioned the cleansing of the temple appointing God-fearing men to handle the duties but then something is brought to him:

> *When they were bringing out the money which had been brought into the house of the LORD, Hilkiah the priest found the book of the law of the LORD given by Moses. Hilkiah responded and said to Shaphan the scribe, "I have found the book of the law in the*

house of the LORD." And Hilkiah gave the book to Shaphan. Then Shaphan brought the book to the king and reported further word to the king, saying, "Everything that was entrusted to your servants they are doing. They have also emptied out the money which was found in the house of the LORD, and have delivered it into the hands of the supervisors and the workmen." Moreover, Shaphan the scribe told the king saying, "Hilkiah the priest gave me a book." And Shaphan read from it in the presence of the king (2 Chronicles 34:14-18).

Some have read this passage and speculated on what book this actually is, but from this verse and *2 Kings 23:25*, we know this is the Pentateuch, the first five books of our modern Bible handed down by Moses.

The importance of the Law is that without such a book, the king did not have a frame of reference for what pleased God. This is the heart of what Paul says in *Romans 7:7*:

What shall we say then? Is the Law sin? May it never be! On the contrary, I would not have come to know sin except through the Law; for I would not have known about coveting if the Law had not said, "YOU SHALL NOT COVET."

Josiah's Sanctification

It did not matter how sincere Josiah had become up to this point, the objective standard for his conduct before God was the Word, and now they have it! The king hears the words of the book and repents. He tore his clothes, which in that time period was a mark of true sadness and humility:

> *When the king heard the words of the law, he tore his clothes. Then the king commanded Hilkiah, Ahikam the son of Shaphan, Abdon the son of Micah, Shaphan the scribe, and Asaiah the king's servant, saying, "Go, inquire of the LORD for me and for those who are left in Israel and in Judah, concerning the words of the book which has been found; for great is the wrath of the LORD which is poured out on us because our fathers have not observed the word of the LORD, to do according to all that is written in this book. (2 Chronicles 34:19-21)*

Not only did Josiah become saddened over the state of the nation, but he also sought to earnestly hear a message from the one true God. This humble repentance is a stark contrast to Josiah's wicked son, Jehoiakim, who burnt the words of God instead (Jeremiah 36:23). Josiah sends for a prophetess to explain the message further and to seek direct counsel.

The prophetess Huldah gave a message of mercy. The king, upon finding the Law, humbled himself before it and allowed himself to be taught by God. While the message returned was not that God would totally withdraw judgment, the king would live in peace because of his response (*2 Chronicles 34:22-28*).

Objective Truth

We started this chapter asking about objective truth. Some people want to believe we all go to heaven as long as we are 'sincere'. What is sincerity anyway? Sincere means to be free of hypocrisy and adulteration, or put another way, to be pure and without false motive[4]. So to be sincere in what you believe means you do not have ulterior motives and you are following what you believe. This is truly a modern message. How many songs, movies, children's programs teach the ubiquitous message, "follow your heart". It sounds wonderful, powerful, and perfect. To yourself be true, they say. But we as people are impacted by the fall. We are never without adulteration nor are we completely pure. We are all fallen beings! Consider that Jeremiah wrote:

Josiah's Sanctification

> *The heart is more deceitful than all else*
> *And is desperately sick;*
> *Who can understand it?*
> *(Jeremiah 17:9)*

In a world where we cannot be pure and unadulterated we need to seek a source of truth outside ourselves and that is exactly what the Bible is. At every turn it has been demonstrated to be scientifically true, historically accurate, and name me a book that can change a heart as wretched as mine to such a degree that I actually started loving people! The Bible is objective truth!

Now we have such truth, the best thing we can do is spend time reading it and allowing it to transform our heart. We will not expound on this now as this is the topic of our next chapter. Presently, we want to understand how Josiah started following God, but without outside direction he was unable to steer the kingdom into the right path. The Law of Moses in his hand helped him to objectively see the required path for the kingdom.

As for us now, find your book! Search your house high and low to find the Bible that has been lost in the mess of your busy life. Now that you have cleaned up the idolatrous clutter from your life and removed the opportunity to sin, dust off that Bible and read it.

See the sin in your life and how you have not been following God. Weep and repent before Him and seek to honor him from this day forward. Allow Him into every place in your heart and start by opening up the pages of your Word and allow it to cut into your sinful desires. Turn back to Him who at once called you. He desires your fellowship and is waiting for you to take the steps to open up to Him:

> *Behold, I stand at the door and knock; if anyone hears My voice and opens the door, I will come in to him and will dine with him, and he with Me. He who overcomes, I will grant to him to sit down with Me on My throne, as I also overcame and sat down with My Father on His throne (Revelation 3:20-21).*

Chapter Summary

Josiah believed he was following God before they found the Law. He was doing what he knew was right but he also did not have all of the story yet. What he was doing was honoring to God, but it was not enough

Josiah's Sanctification

to be sincere, he also had to obey. Once he found the law, he had his eyes opened to how short his work for the Lord was; how it could not satisfy an angry God.

Likewise, we need to focus on Him not through feelings, emotions, or Christian radio, but by digging into the Word! The Bible is the ultimate source of objective truth in our lives and it is very clear many of us do not spend time with God through the pages of Scripture. **Rediscover your Bible** and take time today to start reading and reflecting on the Word.

5
Changing Hearts

But I will leave among you
A humble and lowly people,
And they will take refuge in the name of the LORD.
The remnant of Israel will do no wrong
And tell no lies,
Nor will a deceitful tongue
Be found in their mouths;
For they will feed and lie down
With no one to make them tremble.
Zephaniah 3:12-13

A humble heart is what God most desires in our spirit. King Saul thought He wanted sacrifice but learned the hard way how wrong he was (*1 Samuel*

Josiah's Sanctification

15:13-23). Even David learned obedience is better than sacrifice:

> *For You do not delight in sacrifice,*
> *otherwise I would give it;*
> *You are not pleased with burnt offering.*
> *The sacrifices of God are a broken spirit;*
> *A broken and a contrite heart,*
> *O God, You will not despise.*
> *Psalm 51:16-17*

Even in the New Testament we are commanded to draw near to God in obedience and to humble ourselves in His presence (*James 4:8-10*). But as we humble ourselves, sincere faith only goes so far. The citizens of Judah were delayed heartache of exile because the king became humble, but that was not the end of Josiah's story.

Josiah's Response

Up to this point we have seen Josiah start following God, hear a message from a prophet, and begin cleaning the old worship out of the land. During the cleanup procedures, the Law of Moses was discovered. This would have been the first time people have seen the written law in several decades; probably since the time of Hezekiah, the king's great-grandfather. As God's commands are read to the king he rented his clothing and sought to hear directly from a prophet. Hilkiah, the high priest, sought the prophetess Huldah for a message from God about the lost book. Huldah gives Josiah a bitter-sweet declaration starting with judgment:

> Tell the man who sent you to Me, "Behold, I am bringing evil on this place and on its inhabitants, even all the curses written in the book which they have read in the presence of the king of Judah. Because they have forsaken Me and have burned incense to other gods, that they might provoke Me to anger with all the works of their hands; therefore My wrath will be poured out on this place and it shall not be quenched (2 Chronicles 34:24-25)".

Josiah knew what was coming, and why. We never see him plead with God like Hezekiah (*2 Kings 20:1-3*), but he simply sought to follow the Word they discovered. It was his humility before God, the same humility that spared Nineveh a generation earlier (*Jonah 3:6-10*), and which his grandfather, Manasseh, had discovered at the end of his life (*2 Chronicles 33:12-13*), that caused God to temporarily withdraw

Josiah's Sanctification

His hand from the impending judgment awaiting the rest of His people. Huldah continues:

> But to the king of Judah who sent you to inquire of the LORD, thus you will say to him, 'Thus says the LORD God of Israel regarding the words which you have heard, Because your heart was tender and you humbled yourself before God when you heard His words against this place and against its inhabitants, and because you humbled yourself before Me, tore your clothes and wept before Me, I truly have heard you,' declares the LORD. 'Behold, I will gather you to your fathers and you shall be gathered to your grave in peace, so your eyes will not see all the evil which I will bring on this place and on its inhabitants (2 Chronicles 34:26-28).'

Josiah takes this message and lets go of his sincerity to instead follow the dictates of the law. What started with cleaning out the old idolatry based on hearing the words of judgment ended with finding the Word and putting into the practice all the things God delivered to Moses for all Israel to practice.

His first task after hearing the mercy from Huldah was to gather the elders of the country and make sure they heard the Law (*2 Chronicles 34:29-30*). The words included prescribed worship and sacrifices, the various feasts including the most important Feast of the Passover, and of course the elders were the ones charged with encouraging the people in their families to obey the Law.

Next, we see Josiah himself dedicate himself to following the specific commandments laid out in the book. The elders with him were also made to dedicate themselves to follow the prescriptions delivered by Moses:

> *Then the king stood in his place and made a covenant before the LORD to walk after the LORD, and to keep His commandments and His testimonies and His statutes with all his heart and with all his soul, to perform the words of the covenant written in this book. Moreover, he made all who were present in Jerusalem and Benjamin to stand with him. So the inhabitants of Jerusalem did according to the covenant of God, the God of their fathers (2 Chronicles 34:31-32).*

Every time we find great blessing in Israel it is a result of following the law. Read through the cycles of judges from that book and we see people strayed from the prescribed worship, fell into subjection to their neighbors, and cried out to God. He would send a

Josiah's Sanctification

judge to them who would not only deliver the people from their enemies, but also turn the hearts of people back to God.

King David followed the statutes of God and passed the knowledge to his son, Solomon which he practiced for the first half of his reign. We find the small packets of righteous kings in the history of the divided kingdoms including Asa, Joash, and Hezekiah. These kings all turned back to some degree to follow God, though not as completely as Josiah.

Even after the period of the kings, as Jerusalem lay in ruins, the priest Ezra begins the process of rebuilding the city and the temple. He is joined by Nehemiah and the two complete the work, rebuilding the city walls and the temple. The dedication is a revival beginning with the Word:

> *And all the people gathered as one man at the square which was in front of the Water Gate, and they asked Ezra the scribe to bring the book of the law of Moses which the LORD had given to Israel. Then Ezra the priest brought the law before the assembly of men, women and all who could listen with understanding, on the first day of the seventh*

month. He read from it before the square which was in front of the Water Gate from early morning until midday, in the presence of men and women, those who could understand; and all the people were attentive to the book of the law (Nehemiah 8:1-3).

Reform in our heart always begins with hearing the Word and then putting into practice the things we have learned.

Josiah's Reform

Following God during the period of the Old Testament kings was a very rigid and prescribed life. Just like our time period, it is difficult to do what we know we must, but unlike our time, it was simpler to know exactly what was to be done to please God. He commanded through Moses exactly how and when to worship. Josiah considered this important and began from the very beginning. The most important feast in the Jewish life is the Passover: the commemoration of when the Hebrew nation was freed from Egypt. The first of the reforms we find is the restoration of this most important feast (*2 Chronicles 35:1*).

Josiah's Sanctification

But worship was not an occasional event. The temple was to be staffed by priests who carried out the daily sacrifices and rituals and the Levites who assisted in the work. Josiah saw to those requirements by appointing the priests and Levites according to the requirements in the law (*Numbers 18, 2 Chronicles 35:2-3*).

After the temple was prepared and the Passover began, the king instituted the required sacrifices to the land, even contributing animals for the sacrifice and celebrations; at this point it is important to understand these sacrifices were often feasts during which the people, the priests, Levites, and neighbors celebrated the Lord one with another.

The feast was celebrated in the eighteenth year of his reign when he was 26 years old. This means it took Josiah ten years of growth in the Lord to bring his life in alignment with the Word. This is what incubation means: he was not living like a Carnal Christian: professing salvation but never growing. He also was not accepting some emotional message and 'knowing he is going to heaven' without any impact on his life.

He was progressively growing in Christ. He longed to do what is right and as revelation was brought to him, he was obedient to the Word. That is the greatest lesson we can learn from Josiah.

While his reforms prevented the immediate exile of his people, Josiah did not leave a lasting legacy as thirteen years later he dies in battle leaving his kingdom to a wicked son who quickly converted the nation back to idolatry:

> *They will not lament for him:*
> *'Alas, my brother!' or, 'Alas, sister!'*
> *They will not lament for him:*
> *'Alas for the master!' or, 'Alas for his splendor!'*
> *"He will be buried with a donkey's burial,*
> *Dragged off and thrown out beyond the gates of Jerusalem.*
> *Go up to Lebanon and cry out,*
> *And lift up your voice in Bashan;*
> *Cry out also from Abarim,*
> *For all your lovers have been crushed.*
> *I spoke to you in your prosperity;*
> *But you said, 'I will not listen!'*
> *This has been your practice from your youth,*
> *That you have not obeyed My voice.*
> *The wind will sweep away all your shepherds,*
> *And your lovers will go into captivity;*
> *Then you will surely be ashamed and humiliated*
> *Because of all your wickedness.*
> *You who dwell in Lebanon,*
> *Nested in the cedars,*

Josiah's Sanctification

> *How you will groan when pangs come upon you,*
> *Pain like a woman in childbirth!*
> *Jeremiah 22:18-23*

Josiah's sons would not follow his practices and so from the mouth of Jeremiah a final declaration of conquest is given to the unrepentant people of Judah. If they continued in His Law they may have been spared, but they did not, and so they were judged. God does not take disregard for His Law lightly. He did not during the reign of the kings, and He does not in our New Testament period:

> *And just as they did not see fit to acknowledge God any longer, God gave them over to a depraved mind, to do those things which are not proper, being filled with all unrighteousness, wickedness, greed, evil; full of envy, murder, strife, deceit, malice; they are gossips, slanderers, haters of God, insolent, arrogant, boastful, inventors of evil, disobedient to parents, without understanding, untrustworthy, unloving, unmerciful; and although they know the ordinance of God, that those who practice such things are worthy of death, they not only do the same, but also give hearty approval to those who practice them (Romans 1:28-32).*

What Is Salvation?

As we navigate our Christian lives in our modern era it raises that question of sincerity. We saw Josiah turned to God as a teenager but it took about ten years before he completely put the law back into practice in his kingdom. We need to have the same degree of grace for believers. They will not immediately become mature Christians, but progress in the faith will be evident in their lives.

Salvation is marked by one who repents of the world's ways of living and thinking. They will start to see the ways the culture is not in alignment with God and begin to live differently, but that will only come when we transform our minds (*Romans 12:2*). In other words, when we are saved we long to be taught the Word, but we only grow when we actually do it.

This is what we see in the life of Josiah. He definitely came to a saving knowledge in God, but he was unsure of what that meant in the long-term scope of life. It was when the Law was discovered we see the king truly becoming right with Him. It took the prophets to tell him to follow that Book and then him learning what was in the Law. We have the same command today:

You, however, continue in the things you have learned and become convinced of, knowing from whom you have learned them, and that from childhood you have known the sacred writings which are able to give you the wisdom that leads to salvation through faith which is in Christ Jesus. All Scripture is inspired by God and profitable for teaching, for reproof, for correction, for training in righteousness; so that the man of God may be adequate, equipped for every good work (2 Timothy 3:14-17).

It is our imperative as Christians to open up our Bible and start learning. There are many methods of study we should all use throughout the week; do not forsake any of these, but find out how to put them into practice as a habit.

First, we need to gain a broad overview of the whole Bible, so I recommend reading the whole thing at least once every year. This can be a daunting task, but bring this to prayer as you begin. You can start as I do at Genesis and read all the way through to Revelation. Another option is many Bibles have an annual reading plan in the back which gives you the specific texts jumping from book to book getting you an overview through history, prophecy, and New Testament principles. Another method is to print out a plan for a chronological read through, so you would effectively be reading the book in the order they were written in history. It does not matter which of these you will do, but pick one and start today. A brief warning: the first few times you read the Bible through as a fast overview you will not understand much of it; do not worry, and do not dwell on trying to understand just keep going and after a few years the knowledge and concepts will start to make sense.

Second, find some time a few times per week for a personal devotion. I do not recommend this for every day, but rather a planned once or twice per week. This is the time to seek to understand. Your topics could be looking up verses that interest you for a deep dive study or those passages in your annual read through you did not understand. The best method for these studies include a Chain Reference Bible where verses are linked in footnotes in such a way you can find related verses easily. Another method is to find a Christian book on the topic you are studying and read it slowly with your Bible digesting all the passages and related passages according to the author's outline.

Third, find a good study where someone else is teaching so you can focus on learning from perspectives you may not think about. These can be Sunday school classes at your church, a small group Bible study in your church, or a group of people you learn from independently. My only warning here is to make sure your studies are centered around the Bible, not a video series or a book. Such resources are excellent in some cases, but not for our dedicated Bible studies in fellowship.

Finally, pray! Pray for direction before your studies and that God would teach you something every time you sit down to study. Pray the words you are reading back to Him and seek to understand. Our ultimate directive is not just to academically know the Bible, but to allow it to transform our life. Pray as David did in *Psalm 139:23-24*:

Changing Hearts

Search me, O God, and know my heart;
Try me and know my anxious thoughts;
And see if there be any hurtful way in me,
And lead me in the everlasting way.

Chapter Summary

Josiah humbled himself before the Lord. When the Law was brought to him, he heard it without pride. He tore his clothes and began a reform that lasted a few years finally culminating in the restoration of the Passover and the other required feasts. It was this humility which withheld God's wraith on the people and led to a prosperous kingdom.

The written word caused him to reflect on the kingdom and he saw sincerity was not enough: the Law must be followed! He reformed the kingdom starting with himself and the elders and put into practice everything handed down from Moses. He earned peace in his lifetime and delayed the inevitable.

We are likewise called to follow the Word. We have the benefit of having the complete canon, something Josiah did not have. It is important we devote time every day to read His Word and incorporate it into our lives. Spend time in the Bible and pray for understanding that we may please God in our daily lives. **The Bible is our way of hearing from God, and we need to use the Word to change our hearts.**

6
Planning to Grow

At that time I will bring you in,
Even at the time when I gather you together;
Indeed, I will give you renown and praise
Among all the peoples of the earth,
When I restore your fortunes before your eyes,
Zephaniah 3:20

Left to our natural state and devices we are lost. We have no hope without Christ and no direction without the Word. In our study from the life of Josiah we have seen a king defer God's judgment by humbling himself to the Master's message through prophets and the newly discovered Book of the Law.

Stages Of Faith

As we become believers whether in our youth, an adult, or in our old age, we need to repent. Without agreeing with God that our ways are sinful, there is no hope for us. But just because we genuinely became a Christian it does not mean we are instantly, perfectly sanctified. It is a process marked by distinct phases: babies, young men, and fathers are described by the apostle John:

> *I am writing to you, little children, because your sins have been forgiven you for His name's sake. I am writing to you, fathers, because you know Him who has been from the beginning. I am writing to you, young men, because you have overcome the evil one. I have written to you, children, because you know the Father. I have written to you, fathers, because you know Him who has been from the beginning. I have written to you, young men, because you are strong, and the word of God abides in you, and you have overcome the evil one (1 John 2:12-14).*

By the grace of this passage we see how we live our life is a matter of our stage in Christian growth. As we have said earlier, we deny a person can be saved yet never grow, but that all who come to a saving faith in Christ will grow, starting immediately but slowly.

There is no specific clear boundary between these phases mentioned by John, but we will endeavor a general explanation. Little children as John calls them would best be defined as a person who is brand new in the faith. Like an infant in our physical world, this young believer does not know the difference between good doctrine and bad; they cannot determine what is a "good, Bible believing church" and the cult down the street. They do not know what is good and bad spiritual food. Such a young person, like a child, knows only some basics: There is a heavenly Father, Jesus died for our sins, and we are to obey Him (*1 John 2:1-6*). The little children need spiritual parents. Mentors, elders, and pastors are to help guide them to read and study the Scriptures, to discern sound doctrines and to consume spiritually good content.

Young men would best be understood as late teenagers. They are generally able to stand on their own but do not have a solid understanding of the deeper things of grace. They are people who have stood toe-to-toe with evil forces, have looked into the face of their sin, and turned around to follow Jesus instead. A young man is studied and knowledgeable in the Word and their Bible gives them the strength to go into the world (*1 John 2:13-14*).

A father as defined here are those who have had their battles, and now teach their victories and steadfastness to the next generation as a grandfather to his grandchildren. The fathers of the faith are concerned with deeper knowledge, of what we might call wisdom. They demonstrate more grace than a young man as they have their battle scars yet remain faithful to Christ as He has remained faithful to them (*1 John 2:13-14*).

It is a sad reality that in our present Evangelical age, many churches have set aside the concern for studying the Bible and have thus emasculated their church members. We are like the people described by the author of Hebrews:

> *Concerning him we have much to say, and it is hard to explain, since you have become dull of hearing. For though by this time you ought to be teachers,*

you have need again for someone to teach you the elementary principles of the oracles of God, and you have come to need milk and not solid food. For everyone who partakes only of milk is not accustomed to the word of righteousness, for he is an infant. But solid food is for the mature, who because of practice have their senses trained to discern good and evil (Hebrews 5:11-14).

The body of Christ is presently malnourished and we need to grow strong by learning what the Bible tells us to do. Start today by spending some time in prayer and then open up the Bible and start hearing from the God of the universe.

Slow Growth

My personal experience was slow Christian growth marked by lingering sins and patchwork repairs. I was a genuine believer, captured by Christ at His will. Having a conversion that did not directly involve a friend, family member, or local church, I was not subject to the regular activities present in Evangelical churches at the time, but I recognized the importance of the Word. I started by reading the Bible that was given to me four years eariler and within a year or two

Josiah's Sanctification

I muscled my way through the tome. It was only about a year later when I would eventually start regularly attending my first home church.

The growth in that period was slow. I did not regularly listen to sermons and the few Christian books I found were full of some damning doctrines, but also in that time period I started reading *Foundations of the Christian Faith*[5]. The book showed me the basics of the faith and coupled with Sunday school and the Bible, I was slowly learning what it meant to be a Christian. It was a few years later when my pastor delivered a sermon on Josiah when I began ridding my life of the garbage that plagued me.

This process took about three years for me. It will take some time for you as well, though there is no specific time frame for our incubation period. In Josiah's case we saw it was eight years time between when he first started walking with God and when he started to clean up the kingdom. We need not be concerned with the time it takes to reach this point when our outward growth bursts forth, but start today putting truth into your mind:

Planning to Grow

Be transformed by the renewing of your mind, so that you may prove what the will of God is, that which is good and acceptable and perfect (Romans 12:2).

Be Prayerful

As we begin our walk with God, we must do it in prayer. It is interesting to me that prayer is not mentioned in the life of Josiah, though future studies in this series will focus more on prayer as it was deeply important in the life of his great-grandfather Hezekiah among other kings we will study.

What we do see from his life, however, is consultation with other prophets. We know of three regional prophets to Judah at the time. Huldah was the prophetess Josiah directly consulted when the Book of the Law was discovered. We also know Zephaniah was a contemporary, and relative to the king, so it is curious why he was not the one consulted. Also, Jeremiah began his preaching in the twelfth year of Josiah's reign, though we do not have any specific interaction between the two. For completeness we will mention Nahum also prophesied at this time but he

Josiah's Sanctification

was preaching in Assyria. Also, Habakkuk preached at the end of Josiah's reign but little else is known of him.

The connection to praying in our day and seeking a prophet in the times of the kings is while praise and prayer were always an important part of worship, it was usually through a prophet that kings would seek God's will in certain matters (*1 Samuel 9:9*). This was because the Bible was not yet canonized, we did not have the complete book as we do now.

After the resurrection of Christ, the apostles were given the authority to compile the rest of the Scriptures and create the full canon of the Bible we have now. In this, we get most of our direction from the Bible, but we also have access to God through prayer without a human mediator:

> *Therefore, since we have a great high priest who has passed through the heavens, Jesus the Son of God, let us hold fast our confession. For we do not have a high priest who cannot sympathize with our weaknesses, but One who has been tempted in all things as we are, yet without sin. Therefore let us draw near with confidence to the throne of grace, so that we may receive mercy and find grace to help in time of need (Hebrews 4:14-16).*

We start our plan in prayer seeking to learn from Him through the Bible as we go through our studies.

Remove Old Sin

In the kingdom Josiah inherited, the people were wicked, committing damning worship on every green hill. They were worshiping false gods and even filled the temple with idolatrous objects of worship. In cleaning the kingdom, Josiah had to do away with the opportunity to sin. The idols and poles needed to come down and he even took the pagan priests and sacrificed them as the last burnt offerings upon their alters before smashing those, grinding the objects into dust, and sprinkling it upon gravestones. Josiah cleaned up the kingdom.

Likewise we need to spend time figuring out what is causing us to stumble. If pornography is upon your devices, delete that stuff and install a filter. Confess your sin to a brother or sister in Christ and have them set the passwords for your internet filters so you cannot tinker around in the settings. Examine your movies and music for anything that may not be

Josiah's Sanctification

pleasing to God and get rid of detestable entertainment. I wrote an entire book on this topic called *I AM not amused*[6] which will help you figure out how to honor God in your entertainment. Sometimes moving on means letting go of the past. Get rid of sentimental devices that only serve a purpose to remember the past. That is gone and the world will pass away, but the glorious future is eternity in Christ. If you have bad relationships that always go to sinful places, cut those off entirely. There is no need to be diplomatic in cases of egregious sin.

Our actions often need to be cleaned up as well. The best place to go in the Bible is the latter half of *Ephesians*. Paul gives us five practical points to consider in *Ephesians 4:25-32*: Speak the truth in love, stop stealing, do not sin in anger, do not speak insults, be kind to one another. These are excellent starting points to grow in our sanctification.

Spirit Filled Clean House

Josiah cleaned his kingdom first with cleaning out the sinful things the prophets spoke of, but then by actively adding the required means and objects of worship. We do not have such a prescribed place and ritual of worship, but we do have a Bible that commands us to conduct ourselves in the proper way:

> *Walk no longer just as the Gentiles also walk, in the futility of their mind, being darkened in their understanding, excluded from the life of God because of the ignorance that is in them, because of the hardness of their heart (Ephesians 4:17-18)*

This is not the end of the book or the chapter, but rather, near the beginning. For people who want to say following Jesus means there are no rules of conduct, I will ask them to study the Scriptures. The remainder of the book of Ephesians is about the various practices that are the mark of Christians: Godly conduct, service, obedience. These do not save us; they are the mark we are saved.

We are to know what is in the Bible and place those things into practice. If we do not understand the Word, we cannot follow the Word, and if we do not follow the Word, we may find ourselves like one of the poor wretches who believe they are going to heaven, but Jesus says they are strangers to Him:

Josiah's Sanctification

> *Not everyone who says to Me, 'Lord, Lord,' will enter the kingdom of heaven, but he who does the will of My Father who is in heaven will enter. Many will say to Me on that day, 'Lord, Lord, did we not prophesy in Your name, and in Your name cast out demons, and in Your name perform many miracles?' And then I will declare to them, 'I never knew you; DEPART FROM ME, YOU WHO PRACTICE LAWLESSNESS (MATTHEW 7:21-23).'*

It would be a terrifying day to believe we are saved but find that Jesus Himself says He does not know us! Re-read that section and reflect. This was like Josiah before he found the Book of the Law: he thought he was doing the correct things but even his best cleanup was still a filthy mess to God. Likewise, when we attempt to approach our Christian life out of sincerity, we miss the mark. It is by the sacrifice of Jesus that we are saved, and it is by the Word that we understand who He is and what that means for us today.

Finally, we cannot just do these steps in our own power. Sure, we can try to excise sin from our life on our own strength but we will fail. We can make the house perfect, declutter our life, clean out all the dusty closets, but if we are not indwelt with the Holy Spirit we will fall again:

> Now when the unclean spirit goes out of a man, it passes through waterless places seeking rest, and does not find it. Then it says, 'I will return to my house from which I came'; and when it comes, it finds it unoccupied, swept, and put in order. Then it goes and takes along with it seven other spirits more wicked than itself, and they go in and live there; and the last state of that man becomes worse than the first. That is the way it will also be with this evil generation (Matthew 12:43-45).

Josiah followed God, cleaned up his kingdom, obeyed the voice of God, and placed the Word at the center of his life. This resulted in God withholding judgment and granting mercy instead. If we as believers are going to start seeing the power of God in our lives, we likewise need to cast off the worldly ways and dedicate ourselves to Him. **Become transformed through the Word.**

Create Your Personal Plan

The applications from this little book are quite simple but very profound. Josiah learned in his walk with God that sincerity is not enough: the Word is the ultimate truth for pleasing God. We are also in that same situation and when we take the time to put these principles into practice, our Christian life will be full of joy and blessing. Use this guide to create a plan for your personal sanctification.

The First Steps

Are you saved? If you are unsure of your salvation, begin by understanding your natural inclinations are to sin which separates you from God. If you confess you are powerless over your sin and you believe God has made a way through the sacrifice of

Jesus on the cross for your sins, than place faith in Him.

- ❖ Place your trust in Christ.
- ❖ Find a Bible you can read and understand
- ❖ Identify a place and time to spend time studying

Incubate Your Faith

Growing takes time. It will take some time to grow in Christ and it starts with dedicated study. Learn from your Bible, join in with other Christians in real fellowship, and reflect over your life as it relates to the Scripture. This period of time is growth. You should become more like Christ, but it will take some time to mature as a believer.

- ❖ Look over your life and identify lingering sin
- ❖ Remove the temptations to sin
- ❖ Work on breaking bad habits
- ❖ Make a habit of daily Scripture reading

Create Your Personal Plan

Hear From God

When you are confident your habits are aligning with Scripture and you have cast off the old life for the new, including the practice of your faith, you should start looking for where to serve Christ. We are to follow Him in obedience to spread the Gospel and good deeds.

- ❖ Begin praying for a ministry
- ❖ Seek opportunities to serve Christ
- ❖ Continue in Christian fellowship
- ❖ Find someone to mentor in the faith

The Gospel

We have all sinned. In our natural condition, we perform actions displeasing to God. These actions are called sin, and since God cannot be in the presence of sin, we are, by our nature, separated from Him. If we die in this state, we are bound to eternal separation in hell. However, God provided a way out of our deathly state. Jesus Christ, who was fully God and fully man, lived on the earth, was tempted in all ways as we are, and lived a perfect life. Jesus willingly went to a cross and died for our sins so we would be able to be in the presence of God. This sacrifice by Jesus is a free gift that makes us clean before Him.

Josiah's Sanctification

We take hold of this gift by prayer. We must understand and admit our sinful state, incapable of being able to resist sin. We must acknowledge Jesus has the power to cover our sin. Pray to God to receive Christ's sacrifice on your behalf and you will be cleansed of your sin, both great and small.

If you have prayed to receive Jesus, mind the words in this book. Begin to read the Bible, search out Christian fellowship, and learn what God would teach you. Grow in faith and sanctification, cleanse your heart and submit to God's Word. Welcome to the kingdom.

Bibliography

1. *Studying and Learning*, Max Meenes, 1954, Random House
2. *An Adult Child's Guide to What's "Normal"*, John and Linda Friel, 1990, Health Communications, Inc.
3. *Do Not Create Unnecessary Stumbling Blocks to the Christian Faith*, Randal Rauser, The Christian Post, March 27, 2019
4. Dictionary.com as accessed April 2, 2019
5. *Foundations of the Christian Faith*, James Montgomery Boice, 1986, Intervarsity Press
6. *I AM not amused*, Thomas Murosky, 2019, Our Walk in Christ Publishing

Scripture Index

New Testament....................
- 1 Corinthians 3............29
- 1 John 2.................76pp.
- 1 Thessalonians 4.......11
- 2 Corinthians 11.........14
- 2 Timothy 3...........13, 70
- Acts 19........................45
- Ephesians 4..............84p.
- Hebrews 10.................44
- Hebrews 4...................82
- Hebrews 5...................79
- James 4.......................60
- James 5.......................33
- John 14....................13p.
- Luke 14.......................37
- Matthew 12.................87
- Matthew 7...................86
- Revelation 3................57
- Romans 10.........30, 41p.
- Romans 12............69, 81
- Romans 7....................53

Old Testament.....................
- 1 Samuel 15................59
- 1 Samuel 9..................82
- 2 Chronicles 33..........61
- 2 Chronicles 34. .24, 27, 38, 43, 53pp., 61pp.
- 2 Chronicles 35........65p.
- 2 Kings 18............25, 46
- 2 Kings 20...................61
- 2 Kings 21...................26
- 2 Kings 23...................53
- Isaiah 36.....................25
- Jeremiah 17................56
- Jeremiah 22................68
- Jeremiah 36................54
- Jonah 3.......................61
- Judges 21...................24
- Nehemiah 8................65
- Numbers 18................66
- Numbers 21................25
- Zephaniah 1. 24, 29, 36, 43
- Zephaniah 3. 28, 49, 59, 75

Other Books by Thomas Murosky

I AM not amused
ISBN:
978-1-7325696-2-1 (s)
978-1-7325696-3-8 (e)

Does your entertainment honor God?

Testing and Temptations
ISBN:
978-1-7325696-0-7 (s)
978-1-7325696-1-4 (e)

Do you know what it takes to live like Jesus?

The Art of Shallow Neighboring
ISBN:
978-1976226519 (s)
ASIN:
B076647JZS (e)

How shallow of a neighbor are you?

About Thomas Murosky

Thomas Murosky has a background in Biological Sciences earning his Bachelors in Biochemistry and his Doctorate in Molecular Toxicology. He taught Chemistry at Bucknell University and Western Wyoming Community College. While as a student and professor, Tom worked in several capacities as a children's and youth worker having served the local CEF board, as a counselor for Christian camps, Awana programs, and other youth outreach including a decade of work in Big Brothers, Big Sisters of America.

Tom stepped aside from teaching and academics to work as a technology consultant to focus more time on writing, blogging, and video production in the area of Christian teaching with an emphasis on discipleship and sanctification. His first book, Testing and Temptations, is about how we are called to transform our lives to be like Christ in the process of Sanctification. His second book, The Art of Shallow Neighboring is parody book calling us to better Christian discernment in the books we read. His third book, I AM Not Amused calls for sober analysis of the media entertainment industry. In addition to these, Tom produces videos on current Christian events and sound theology on OurWalkinChrist on YouTube.

You can find more information and other books Thomas has authored at www.ourwalkinchrist.com. Signup for the newsletter for information on future releases, promotions, and advance reader copies at www.ourwalkinchrist.com/newsletter.

www.ingramcontent.com/pod-product-compliance
Lightning Source LLC
Chambersburg PA
CBHW022213090526
44584CB00013BA/841